NEWPORT (R.I.)
The Delaplaine
2015
Long Weekend Guide

Andrew Delaplaine

**NO ONE HAS PAID A SINGLE PENNY OR GIVEN *ANYTHING*
TO BE INCLUDED IN THIS BOOK.**

A list of the author's other travel guides, as well as his political thrillers
and titles for children, can be found at the end of this book.

Senior Editors
Renee & Sophie Delaplaine

Senior Writer
James Cubby

Gramercy Park Press

Copyright © by Gramercy Park Press - All rights reserved.
Certain content licensed by Creative Commons per this link:
http://en.wikipedia.org/wiki/Founders%27_Copyright

Please submit corrections, additions or comments to
andrewdelaplaine@mac.com

NEWPORT (R.I.)
The Delaplaine 2015 Long Weekend Guide

TABLE OF CONTENTS

Chapter 1 – WHY NEWPORT? – 4

Chapter 2 – WHERE TO STAY – 9
High on the Hog – Sensible Alternatives – Budget

Chapter 3 – WHERE TO EAT – 19
Extravagant – Middle Ground – Budget

Chapter 4 – NIGHTLIFE – 33

Chapter 5 – WHAT TO SEE & DO – 37

Chapter 6 – NEWPORT'S "COTTAGES" – 46

Chapter 7 – SHOPPING & SERVICES – 49

INDEX – 55

OTHER BOOKS BY THE SAME AUTHOR – 58

Chapter 1
WHY NEWPORT?

There are two wildly divergent sides to Newport that have always fascinated me.

On the one hand you have the quaint cobblestone streets lined with galleries, shops, cafés, stores filled with artisanally-crafted wares, tacky tourist traps, the port area where you're reminded that this was a place as connected to the sea as any weather-beaten town on the Maine Coast.

And then on the other hand, you have the "cottages," as the wealthy robber barons of the Gilded Age quaintly called their mega-mansions that make this town unique in all the world.

Back before the 1920s, you could walk up Fifth Avenue and see humongous townhouses owned by some the same families that built these summer "cottages" in Newport (most of which were occupied only for one or two months a year). Most of these houses were designed in the over-the-top ornate Beaux-Arts style favored at the time, everything, of course, copied from European styles America's wealthy sought to replicate with so much fervor in the eternal struggle to become "respectable."

In Manhattan, however, only a few of these houses remain. The Frick, for instance, at 70th Street and Fifth Avenue, is my personal favorite. Its interiors remain mostly as Henry Clay Frick left them except that they've been converted into galleries to display his vast art collection. Other New York houses, such as Andrew Carnegie's 64-room mansion built in 1902 on Fifth Avenue and 91st Street, have been repurposed as homes for nonprofit cultural institutions. In the Carnegie case, his house in now the Cooper-Hewitt Museum. (I've always found the house much more interesting than the exhibits mounted by Cooper-Hewitt sometimes daffy curators, but that's another story.)

As I was saying, most of the houses lining Fifth Avenue were torn down only a decade or two after they were raised at such great expense. The real estate on Fifth Avenue just became so expensive that the families (after income taxes were introduced) decided to sell out rather than preserve these gorgeous houses an fine examples of period architecture. The big apartment blocks you see now on Fifth Avenue replaced those houses.

In Newport, however, the houses did not come down and a grand effort to preserve them was made. That's why they're here for you to marvel at today. And don't even think about coming to Newport if you don't make time for 2 or 3 of these wonderful houses.

Newport is home to any number of internationally recognized festivals and fairs, primary among them the Newport Folk Festival and the Newport Jazz Festival. Be sure to check out the schedules so you know what's going on during your Long Weekend visit.

Chapter 3
WHERE TO STAY

AIRBNB
www.airbnb.com
Book a room or an entire apartment from an individual. You pay AirBnB and they pay the host after you check in. The good thing here is that you get to review the host (but the host also gets to review you after you leave), and this process works to keep both sides honest.

PRICELINE and **HOTWIRE**
www.priceline.com
www.hotwire.com
With Priceline, you bid on rooms in the part of the city where you want to stay, select whatever star levels you want, and generally can get cheaper rooms. These are usually in hotel chains, so nothing with too much character. With Hotwire, they tell you the price of the room. You don't bid on it. You can often play one site off against the other to get an even cheaper

deal. (You don't find out the name of the lodging until you close the deal.)

ADMIRAL FITZROY INN
398 Thames St, Newport, 866-848-8780
www.admiralfitzroy.com
This premier getaway offers guests deluxe guestrooms in a European-style bed & breakfast. All rooms are decorated with antique sleigh beds and hand-stenciled armoires. Amenities include: free continental breakfast, private phone line, cable TV, small fridge, and free paring. Two-night minimum required most weekends. Conveniently located near local restaurants and shopping.

THE ALMONDY INN
25 Pelham St, Newport, 401-848-7202
www.almondyinn.com
Conveniently located near Bannister's and Bowens Wharfs on Narragansett Bay, this restored 1890's

Victorian inn features five elegant guestrooms and suites decorated with period antiques. Amenities include: Flat screen TV, DVD player, free Wi-Fi, signature bath amenities, free bottled water and daily maid service.

ARCHITECT'S INN
2 Sunnyside Pl, Newport, 401-845-2547
www.architectsinn.com
Constructed in 1873, this palatial guesthouse was originally the private home of George Champlin Mason, the famous Newport architect. Located on "Historic Hill", this Victorian mansion offers beautifully appointed rooms, suites, and studios decorated in period furnishings. Amenities include: free breakfast, free Wi-Fi, free parking, and free breakfast. Massage therapist available. This inn also hosts Murder Mystery Weekends.

CASTLE HILL INN
590 Ocean Dr, Newport, 888-466-1355
www.catlehillinn.com
Located on 40-acre peninsula overlooking the mouth of Narragansett Bay, this restored 1875 mansion offers a variety of luxurious accommodations including a Swiss-style Chalet, Beach houses and cottages with a private beach. Amenities include: free breakfast, free Wi-Fi, and room service.

CLIFFSIDE INN
2 Seaview Ave, Newport, 401-847-1811
www.cliffsideinn.com

Nestled in the center of the historic district, this elegantly restored 1876 Victorian mansion inn offers beautifully designed guest rooms and suites. Conveniently located near local restaurants and shopping districts, this inn offers a beautiful getaway. Amenities include: whirlpool baths, spa showers, grand beds, LCD TVs, DVD players, iPod sound systems, a serene wrap-around porch, free gourmet breakfast, free Wi-Fi, and free parking.

FORTY 1° NORTH
351 Thames St, Newport, 401-846-8018
www.41north.com
This state-of-the-art hotel and marina is one of Newport's newest waterfront destinations boasting both restaurants and lounges. The resort hotel offers excellent accommodations with environmentally friendly amenities. All 28 guest rooms offer amenities like: gas fireplace, iPad, LED 40-inch flat-screen TV,

free Wi-Fi, laptop compatible in-room safe, daily newspapers and desk-integrated media system. The resort features beautiful views of Newport Harbor and Thames Street. In-room spa services available. Pet friendly accommodations available. Valet parking.

MARSHALL SLOCUM GUEST HOUSE
29 Kay St, Newport, 401-841-5120
www.marshallslocuminn.com
Repeatedly named by several publications as "Best Rhode Island Bed and Breakfast," this guesthouse continues to welcome satisfied returning guests. All six rooms are decorated with period antiques with amenities that include: Gilchrist and Soames toiletries, free Wi-Fi, free full morning breakfast, and free parking. Conveniently located just a short walk from downtown Newport and waterfront attractions.

NEWPORT BEACH HOTEL & SUITES
1 Wave Ave, Newport, 401-846-0310
www.newportbeachhotelandsuites.com
Formerly the Inn at Newport Beach, this hotel offers the largest and most luxurious guest rooms in Newport County. Amenities include: 37 inch LCD TV with HD DirecTV, HD DVD/CD player, MP3 player, iPod docking station, free Wi-Fi, and gourmet coffee and teas. Facilities include: indoor pool and whirlpool, fitness center with spa treatment room and rooftop hot tub and firepit. Located steps away from Easton's Beach and near recreation opportunities (skateboard park, aquarium and carousel). Private trainers and fitness instructors available. Free parking. On-site restaurant.

NEWPORT MARRIOTT
25 Americas Cup Ave, Newport, 401-849-1000
www.marriott.com/hotels/travel/pvdlw-newport-marriott
This Marriott offers first-class accommodations including perks like a full-service spa, an indoor pool, fitness center and on-site restaurant. This hotel offers 312 rooms and 7 suites on 7 floors. Amenities include: free Wi-Fi, daily newspaper delivery (on request), 32" HDTV, and a laptop safe. This is a

smoke-free hotel. Conveniently located near beach facilities and sailing and golfing opportunities.

THAMES STREET GUEST HOUSE
15 Thames St (btw Poplar St and Bridge St), Newport, 401-846-8471
www.15thames.com
Originally an 1869 Italianate Victorian home, this Guest House offers luxurious accommodations. Amenities include: free Continental breakfast, Cable TV, DVD, free Wi-Fi, an LED fireplace and air conditioning. Conveniently located near downtown Newport and waterfront/harbor areas. Two-night minimum stay on weekends.

HOTEL VIKING
One Bellevue Ave, Newport, 401-847-3300
www.hotelviking.com
This historic hotel offers a wonderful combination of old with modern comfort and amenities. Facility includes: Fitness Center, pool, spa, salon, Jacuzzi, and two on-site restaurants. Amenities include: free Wi-Fi, morning coffee in lobby and daily coffee in room, flat screen LCD TV, and gourmet honor baskets. Children's activities. Smoke free hotel.

Chapter 4
WHERE TO EAT

22 BOWEN'S WINE BAR AND GRILL
22 Bowen's Wharf, Newport, 401-841-8884
www.22bowens.com
CUISINE: Argentinean
DRINKS: Full Bar
SERVING: Breakfast, Brunch, Late night
PRICE RANGE: $$
This sophisticated eatery offers guests an elegant dining experience with panoramic views of Newport Harbor. Menu favorites include: Atlantic Salmon Fillet and Georges Bank Scallops. Gluten-free menu available. The bar offers an impressive list of wines, beers, lagers and ales.

BELLE'S CAFE
1 Washington St, Newport, 401-846-6000
www.newportshipyard.com/bellescafe.asp
CUISINE: Cafe
DRINKS: No Booze
SERVING: Breakfast, Lunch
PRICE RANGE: $$

Boasting a reputation as the best place for breakfast in town, this café also offers a great lunch menu. Menu favorites include: Stuffed French Toast (breakfast) and Jamaican Jerk Chicken (lunch). Great daily specials. Guests get a great view of the Newport Bridge and can watch the yachts come in and out.

BRICK ALLEY PUB
140 Thames St, Newport, 401 849-6334
www.brickalley.com
CUISINE: American
DRINKS: Full Bar
SERVING: Lunch, Dinner
PRICE RANGE: $$
Here you'll find a comfortable place to dine plus a great menu of "pub style" comfort food, steaks, pizza, pasta, and local seafood. The wine list includes over 250 vintages.
Menu favorites: Buffalo Chicken pizza and Lemony Chicken Piccata. The bar serves an impressive variety of creative cocktails like the Chocolate Mint Cookie, a sweet cocktail with a punch. Gluten-free menu available.

BUSKERS IRISH PUB
178 Thames St, Newport, 401-846-5856
www.buskerspub.com
CUISINE: Irish
DRINKS: Full Bar
SERVING: Breakfast, Brunch, Late night
PRICE RANGE: $$
This old world style pub is decorated with Irish antiques and features live music on weekends. No

longer serving just "pub" food, this place now boasts to be Newport's only gastropub. Menu favorites include: Filet Mignon wrapped in Irish bacon and Goat Cheese & Prosciutto Shrimp.

CLARKE COOKE HOUSE
1 Bannisters Wharf, Newport, 401-849-2900
www.bannistersnewport.com
CUISINE: Seafood, Sushi Bar
DRINKS: Full Bar
SERVING: Lunch, Dinner
PRICE RANGE: $$$
Located in an 18th century building, the Clarke Cooke House offers several dining options. The Porch, an elegant dining room, The Candy Store, a more relaxed dining situation located at harbor level. Intimate cocktails are available at The SkyBar. Menu favorites include: Summer Sushi. The wine list includes over 400 selections, including everything from regional wines to vintage Bordeaux.

THE DECK
1 Waite's Wharf, Newport, 401-846-3600
www.waiteswharf.com
CUISINE: American/Seafood
DRINKS: Full Bar
SERVING: Lunch, Dinner
PRICE RANGE: $$$
This dockside venue offers fine dining, live entertainment, dancing and an outdoor lounge. Menu favorites include: Pan Seared Sea Scallops and Braised Lamb Shank. Great place for seafood lovers and a nightspot for the 20-30 year old crowd.

DIEGO'S MEXICAN RESTAURANT
11 Bowens Wharf, Newport, 401-619-2640
www.diegosnewport.com
CUISINE: Mexican
DRINKS: Full Bar
SERVING: Lunch, Dinner
PRICE RANGE: $$
This casual eatery offers Mexican cuisine with a modern twist. Menu favorites include: Crispy Pork Belly Tacos and Enchilada del Dia (stuffed enchiladas of the day). Try their creative cocktails like the Passion of Spice (El Buho Mezcal, fresh passion fruit puree, Habanero infused tequila, sour and pineapple juice). Gluten-free menu available.

FLUKE WINE BAR & KITCHEN
41 Bowen's Wharf, Newport, 401-849-7778;
www.flukewinebar.com
CUISINE: American

DRINKS: Full Bar
SERVING: Dinner
PRICE RANGE: $$
This casual two-level eatery located on the water offers a fresh creative seasonal menu. Menu favorites include: Roasted Eggplant Puree and Duck Empanaditas. The bar serves creative cocktails and a nice selection of wines.

FIFTH ELEMENT
111 Broadway, Newport, 401-619-2552
www.thefifthri.com
CUISINE: American
DRINKS: Full Bar
SERVING: Dinner
PRICE RANGE: $$
This combination bar and restaurant offers a great dining experience in a casual atmosphere. The cocktail and martini menu is pretty impressive and the food menu is just as creative. Menu favorites include: Spinach Balls and Lamb Kebob Salad.

FRANKLIN SPA
229 Spring St, Newport, 401-847-3540
CUISINE: American
DRINKS: No Booze
SERVING: Breakfast, Lunch
PRICE RANGE: $$
This down-to-earth diner is a breakfast favorite. Open since 1999, this place serves breakfast all day and great lunch selections. Menu favorites include: Lobster omelette and Shared Eggs Benedict. Always busy. Cash only.

MIDTOWN OYSTER BAR
345 Thames St, Newport, 401-619-4100
www.midtownoyster.com
CUISINE: American
DRINKS: Full Bar
SERVING: Lunch, Dinner
PRICE RANGE: $$
This is a top-notch seafood multi-level restaurant with the largest raw bar in Newport. Menu favorites include: Caramelized Sea Scallops and Oven Roasted Twin Lobster Tails. First floor has live music. Very busy.

MOORING SEAFOOD KITCHEN & BAR
1 Sayer's Wharf, Newport, 401-846-2260
www.mooringrestaurant.com
CUISINE: Seafood
DRINKS: Full Bar

SERVING: Breakfast, Lunch, Dinner
PRICE RANGE: $$$
This charming seafood eatery offers an amazing dining experience featuring indoor and outdoor dining. Their wine list features many of New England's best and includes more than 600 labels. Menu favorites include: Croissant Lobster Roll and Portuguese Roasted Cod. Gluten-free menu available. Reservations recommended.

PERRO SALADO
19 Charles St, Newport, 401-619-4777
www.perrosalado.com
CUISINE: Mexican
DRINKS: Full Bar
SERVING: Dinner, Lunch on Sun
PRICE RANGE: $$
This place serves great creative traditional Mexican fare. The portions are large and you won't be disappointed. Menu favorites include: Mexican Scallops and Sticky Ribs. Great margaritas and sangria. Reservations recommended.

POUR JUDGEMENT
32 Broadway, Newport, 401-619-2115
www.pourjudgement.com
CUISINE: American
DRINKS: Full Bar
SERVING: Lunch, Dinner
PRICE RANGE: $$
Popular restaurant among locals, this place offers a creative menu featuring soups, salads, sandwiches, seafood, and pastas. Nice selection of craft beers.

Menu favorites include: Gouda Cheese Fries and Thai Shrimp Curry Nachos.

RED PARROT
348 Thames St, Newport, 401-847-3800
www.redparrotrestaurant.com
CUISINE: American
DRINKS: Full Bar
SERVING: Lunch, Dinner

PRICE RANGE: $$
One of the city's most popular restaurants, this eatery offers an eclectic 20-page menu prepared in two separate kitchens. Located in a historic building, there are three floors of dining and four bars. Menu favorites include: Blackened Mahi Mahi and Mandarin Coconut Chicken. Bar menu features assortment of creative cocktails and frozen drinks. Popular for large parties.

RHINO BAR & GRILLE
337 Thames St, Newport, 401-846-0707
www.redparrotrestaurant.com
CUISINE: American
DRINKS: Full Bar
SERVING: Dinner
PRICE RANGE: $$
This multi-club venue features a sports bar with an extensive menu as well as a nightclub. The bar menu includes a variety of cocktails, martinis, and local beers on tap. Live music.
Menu favorites include: Open-Faced BBQ Pulled Pork Sandwich and Sesame Salmon. Lots of daily specials. This is a unique venue with a variety of entertainment options so you can enjoy live music or dance after dinner.

SPICED PEAR @ THE CHANLER
401-847-2244
www.thechanler.com/dining
CUISINE: Seafood
DRINKS: Full Bar
SERVING: Breakfast, Lunch, Dinner

PRICE RANGE: $$$
Located in the historic Chanler Hotel, this seafood eatery features fireside dining with a romantic terrace. The venue includes an open-air kitchen, grand fireplace, and great ocean views. Known for its signature "New England Tasting menu," guests select from an ever-changing menu featuring local New England fare. Menu favorites include: Free Range Half Chicken and Wild Alaskan King Salmon. Impressive wine list. Live jazz on weekends.

TALLULAH ON THAMES
464 Thames St, Newport, 401-849-2433
www.tallulahonthames.com
CUISINE: American

DRINKS: Full Bar
SERVING: Dinner Closed Mon & Tues
PRICE RANGE: $$$$
This place serves delicious food with a great presentation; some say it's almost too pretty to eat. Menu favorites include: Striped Bass Crudo and Quinoa Crusted Chicken. Nice 4-course tasting menu that's perfect for sharing.

THE WHARF PUB AND RESTAURANT
37 Bowen's Wharf, Newport, 401-846-9233
www.thewharfpubnewport.com
CUISINE: Argentinean
DRINKS: Full Bar
SERVING: Breakfast, Brunch, Late night
PRICE RANGE: $$
Their porch is a popular place to watch the action on Bannister's Wharf however dining inside the cozy dining room is best. The menu of pub food also includes meat, seafood, and pasta entrees. Menu favorites include: Roasted Turkey Meatloaf and BBQ Pork Shoulder Mac N Cheese. There's also a raw bar and a gluten-free menu. The bar offers 28 bottled beers and micro brews and a list of creative cocktails. Live music on Wednesday nights.

WHITE HORSE TAVERN
26 Marlborough St, 401-849-3600
www.whitehorsenewport.com
CUISINE: American
DRINKS: Full Bar
SERVING: Lunch, Dinner
PRICE RANGE: $$$

Built in 1652, this is the oldest bar in the nation. This historic venue offers fine dining in an elegant setting. There are two bars and you must try a Darn and Stormy, the unofficial cocktail of Newport. The Tavern features a contemporary culinary experience with a menu that includes fresh local fish, clams, and lobster. Menu favorites include: Lobster Mac & Cheese and New England Style Crabcake.

Chapter 5
NIGHTLIFE

BOOM BOOM ROOM
Clark Cook House
285 Thames St, Newport, 401-849-2900
www.bannistersnewport.com/clarke_boom_boom.html
Located in the basement of Clark Cook House restaurant, this nightspot offers music and dancing. This popular discotheque is very dark and attracts an eclectic crowd of all ages.

THE FASTNET PUB
1 Broadway, Newport, 401-845-9311
www.thefastnetpub.com
This popular local pub offers a variety of beers on tap, simple but strong cocktails, and a great place to catch the sports games on TV. Like your old-time pubs, this place has dartboards, a pool table, and a back patio for smoking. There's a simple menu of pub fare like fish and chips. Irish music night every Sunday.

JIMMY'S SALOON
37 Memorial Blvd, Newport, 401-846-5121
No Website
A popular local bar for over 25 years, this large saloon features several pool tables, live music and a jukebox. They offer a small menu of bar food. Stop by on Friday night (5-7 p.m.) for free barbeque and live music. There's Karaoke on Saturday nights.

NEWPORT BLUES CAFÉ
286 Thames St, Newport, 401-841-5510
www.newportblues.com/Newport_Blues_Cafe/Home.html
Housed in a historic brownstone built in 1892, this world-class, live music venue offers an impressive roster of local and national acts with a variety of music genres represented including classic rock, blues, progressive, indie rock and hip-hop.

O'BRIEN'S PUB
501 Thames St, Newport, 401-849-6623
www.theobrienspub.com
Located in the fifth ward district of Newport, this pub is a local's favorite for its bar scene but also offers a large menu for lunch and dinner. During summer season, the outdoor garden patio is quite popular and a great place to enjoy cocktails or dinner. The bar offers a variety of video games, pool tables and 5 TVs.

ONE PELHAM EAST
270 Thames St, Newport, 401-847-9460
www.thepelham.com

Open since 1975, this is Newport's oldest rock club. The place has booked its share of celebrity rock and reggae performers and has been a favorite hangout for the America's Cup sailing teams. Live bands and a dance floor. Open 7 nights a week.

Chapter 5
WHAT TO SEE & DO

ADIRONDACK II
23 Bowens Wharf, Newport, 401-847-0000
www.sail-newport.com
Built in 1999 by Scarano Boat Building, this 80-foot boat is representational of a classic turn-of-the-century Pilot Schooner. A cruise aboard the Adirondack II is an experience as it passes Newport's stately bayside mansions, a 19th Century military fort and beautiful old lighthouses. This schooner can accommodate up to 60 passengers. Prices vary depending on the type of cruise. Available for

corporate and private sailing charters, day sails and sunset cruises.

ADVENTURE WATER SPORTS
2 E Ferry Wharf, Jamestown, 401-849-4820
www.newportriwatersports.com
This is your one-stop destination for water activities. Here you can rent jet skis, wave runners, boats, kayaks, and book fishing trips. You can even charter your own yacht for a special cruise. Open daily.

AQUIDNECK GROWERS WEDNESDAY FARMERS MARKET
Memorial Blvd. & Chapel St., Newport, no phone
www.aquidneckgrowersmarket.org
Open every Wednesday (June 4 – October 29, 2 – 6 p.m.) this weekly Farmers Market offers a great marketplace with more than 25 vendors selling both organic and conventionally-grown products including: fresh vegetables, cut flowers, herbs, berries, fruit, plants, eggs, breads, baked goods, meats, seafood, and cheeses. There's also live music.

BRETON POINT STATE PARK
Ocean Drive, Newport
www.riparks.com/Locations/LocationBrentonPoint.html
Occupying the former grounds of one of Newport's grandest estates, this park offers spectacular views as it's located at the point where Narragansett Bay meets the Atlantic Ocean. Visitors can enjoy the view, picnic, hike, and fish. Open year round. No fees.

BRICK MARKET HISTORIC DISTRICT
Brick Market, Newport
www.brickmarketnewport.com
The Newport Historic District covers 250 acres in the center of that city with a selection of intact colonial buildings. The historic buildings include the city's oldest house and the former meeting place of the colonial and state legislatures. Set on Newport's waterfront, this is a favorite tourist attraction.

CLASSIC CRUISES OF NEWPORT
Bannister's Wharf, 401-847-0298
www.cruisenewport.com
Classic Cruises offers a great variety of water entertainment including sailing, powerboat tours and sunset cocktail harbor cruises. Cruises feature spectacular views of Newport Harbor and Narragansett Bay. Choose from a 72' Schooner or a high-speed motor yacht. Modest fees depending on tour.

CLIFF WALK
www.cliffwalk.com
This scenic three and a half mile walkway borders the back lawn of The Breakers and several other beautiful Newport Mansions. This is one of the top attractions in Newport. The walk runs from the east end of Bailey's Beach to the west end of First Beach.

FORT ADAMS
1 Lincoln Dr, Newport, 401-841-0707
www.fortadams.org
This State Park offers panoramic views of Newport Harbor and the East Passage of Narragansett Bay. Park activities include: saltwater bathing, fishing, boating, soccer, rugby, and picnicking. The park is known for its annual summer concerts. Permits needed to play rugby and soccer. Tours available.

INTERNATIONAL TENNIS HALL OF FAME AT THE NEWPORT CASINO
194 Bellevue Ave, Newport, 401-849-3990
www.tennisfame.com

Housed in the historic Newport Casino, this venue celebrates the history of tennis dating from the 12th Century to the present. The Hall of Fame has 18 galleries with over 20,000 square feet of interactive exhibits, videos, and tennis memorabilia. The collection contains over 16,000 objects. Open daily. Nominal admission fee.

JANE PICKENS THEATER
49 Touro St, Newport, 401-846-5252
www.janepickens.com
Located in Washington Square, this world-class art house cinema happens to be one of America's oldest theaters. The theater offers an impressive schedule of films, documentaries, and public events.

MUSEUM OF YACHTING
449 Thames St, Newport, 401-847-1018
www.iyrs.edu/MuseumofYachting
Located in the 1831 Aquideneck Mill, this museum celebrates yachting with informative exhibits,

lectures, literature and regattas. Here you can watch craftsmen build a boat and learn the basic principles of sailing. Open Tues - Sat.

THE *M/V GANSETT*, GANSETT CRUISES
2 Bowens Wharf, Newport, 401-787-4438
www.gansettcruises.com
Cruises aboard the M/V Gansett offer a scenic tour of Newport and Jamestown. One and a half hour narrated harbor tours and sunset cruises available. Both cruises offer cocktails, beer and wine. The M/V Gansett is a well-appointed private yacht manned by well-informed guides. Price varies depending on cruise.

NATIONAL MUSEUM OF AMERICAN ILLUSTRATION
492 Bellevue Ave, Newport, 401-851-8974
www.americanillustration.org
Founded in 1998 by Judy and Laurence S. Cutler to house their art collection, this museum now exhibits art from all periods and styles. The museum building is an interpretation of an 18th century French chateau with three-acre grounds inspire by King Henry VIII's garden. The museum offers one of the greatest collections of American illustrations in perpetuity. Open year-round by advance reservation for group and VIP tours.

NAVAL WAR COLLEGE MUSEUM
686 Cushing Rd, Newport, 401-841-4052
www.usnwc.edu

This museum's exhibitions celebrate the history of naval warfare and the naval heritage of Narragansett Bay. The collection museum offers exhibits pertaining to the genesis of the Navy in the region. Open daily. Reservations necessary made one working day in advance. Non-U.S. Citizens require 14 days advance notice.

NEWPORT ART MUSEUM
76 Bellevue Ave, Newport, 401-848-8200
www.newportartmuseum.org
This museum celebrates Newport and Rhode Island's rich cultural heritage. The museum's permanent collection of over 2,300 works of American art focuses on 19th century to present day featuring artists like Howard Gardiner Cushing, Dale Chihuly, Richard Merking, James Baker, Rita Rogers and Sue McNally.
Nominal admission fee. Closed Mondays.

NEWPORT DISTILLING COMPANY/THOMAS TEW DISTILLERY
Coastal Extreme Brewing Company
293 J. T. Connell Rd, Newport, 401-849-5232
www.newportstorm.com
See firsthand how run is made and taste single barrel rum in the 3 stages of the aging process. The Visitors Center is open everyday (except Tuesdays) for tours and tastings. Visitors can view the distillery from the tour deck or enjoy one of the daily-guided tours (3 p.m.). Reservations not necessary. Nominal admission fee. Group private tours available.

NEWPORT GULLS BASEBALL TEAM
20 Americas Cup Ave, Newport, 401-849-4982
www.newportgulls.com
This is a wooden-bat, summer collegiate baseball team called the Newport Gulls. The team has won several NECBL Championships. Check website for schedule.

NORMAN BIRD SANCTUARY
583 Third Beach Rd, Middletown, 401-846-2577
www.normanbirdsanctuary.org
Established in 1949 at the bequest of Mabel Norman Cerio, this 325-acre sanctuary offers diverse habitats to study birds. Guided bird walks available (every other Sunday beginning at 8 a.m.). Walks are free for members, a nominal fee is charged for non-members.

THE OCEAN DRIVE
www.oceandrivenewport.com
Ocean Drive offers ten miles of historic landmarks and breathtaking views of the Atlantic Ocean. Take RI-138 east or RI-114 south and follow the signs for RI-138A/Memorial Boulevard and turn right on Bellevue Drive heading south and the scenic drive begins.

ROUGH POINT
680 Bellevue Ave, Newport, 401-847-8344
www.newportrestoration.org
This is one of the Gilded Age mansions, formerly the Newport home of heiress Doris Duke; this beautiful oceanfront estate is now open as a museum. Still decorated as the infamous philanthropist and art

collector left it, this mansion is filled with French furniture, European art, Chinese porcelains, and Turkish carpets. Tours last about 75 minutes. Nominal admission fee.

SAMUEL WHITEHORNE HOUSE MUSEUM
416 Thames St, Newport, 401-849-7300
www.newportrestoration.org
This Federal style mansion is open to the public as a historic house museum. The museum contains some of the best examples of Newport and Rhode Island furniture from the late 18th century including examples of craftsmen from the renowned Townsend and Goddard workshops. Open Thursday – Monday. Nominal admission fee, guided tours available.

TOURO SYNAGOGUE NATIONAL HISTORIC SITE
85 Touro St, Newport, 401-847-4794
www.tourosynagogue.org
Built in 1763, the Touro Synagogue is the oldest synagogue still standing in the United States and the only surviving synagogue in the U.S. dating back to the colonial era.
Nominal admission fee. Tours available. Closed on Saturdays.

Chapter 6
NEWPORT'S "COTTAGES"

NEWPORT MANSIONS
The Preservation Society of Newport County
www.newportmansions.org
This is a central website where you can explore some of the houses open to the public and buy tickets good to more than one tour. Houses covered here are:

THE BREAKERS
MARBLE HOUSE
THE ELMS
ROSECLIFF
CHATEAU-SUR-MER
KINGSCOTE
ISAAC BELL HOUSE
GREEN ANIMALS TOPIARY GARDEN
HUNTER HOUSE
CHEPSTOWE

If you only have time for 2 or 3 houses, tour the **Breakers**, the **Elms** and **Rough Point**. Those are my 3 favorites.

Also, if you have the time, I urge you to take the **Service Life Tour** at the Elms. This newly-updated tour will highlight the stories of some of the men and women who worked to service the social whirl of Newport during the Gilded Age. You'll hear the stories of the butler, Ernest Birch; his wife, cook Grace Rhodes; and one of the maids, Nellie Lynch Regoli. Recent research has revealed new details about life behind-the-scenes in the great houses of Newport. Included in the tour is new information about immigration, employment and labor disputes in the early 20th century.

You'll climb the 82 stairs of the back staircase from the basement servant entrance up to the third floor staff quarters, where you'll see exhibits and photographs about the individual men and women who lived and worked here. Weather permitting your tour will take you out onto the roof, for a spectacular view of the ten-acre estate and Newport Harbor beyond. Then, head back down the stairs to the basement kitchens, coal cellar, boiler room and laundry rooms.

Here are some other notable great houses in Newport:

ASTOR BEECHWOOD MANSION
This was the Astor family's summer getaway place, now a privately owned museum.

BELCOURT CASTLE

ORCHRE COURT

ROUGH POINT
Newport Restoration Foundation
www.newportrestoration.org
This foundation was set up by Doris Duke, and it manages **Rough Point,** her oceanfront mansion here. This is definitely a worthy stop on your visit. Duke was the heiress, philanthropist and art collector. Enjoy her magnificent oceanfront estate, still decorated as she left it, where you will see French furniture, European art, Chinese porcelains, and Turkish carpets collected from exotic locations around the world. Located on Newport's exclusive Bellevue Avenue, Rough Point provides a sweeping ocean view and expansive grounds designed by renowned landscape architect Frederick Law Olmsted, whose other little project in his life was designing Central Park in New York.

Chapter 7
SHOPPING & SERVICES

BRAHMIN LEATHER WORKS
22 Bannister's Wharf, Newport, 401-849-5990
www.brahmin.com
This shop sells the handcrafted Brahmin handbag that is both elegant and long lasting. The brand is known worldwide. Here you'll find handbags and accessories.

CABBAGE ROSE
493 Thames St, Newport, 401-846-7006
No website
This local boutique offers unique, original fashions for women. You'll also find a great selection of shoes and jewelry.

COOKIE JAR
29 Bowen's Wharf, Newport, 401-846-5078
www.bowenswharf.com
Since 1977, this little bakery has been selling sweets to locals and visitors. Here you'll find an assortment of fresh muffins, scones, cinnamon rolls, cookies,

breakfast sandwiches, bagels, and banana bread. Of course many come for the vast variety of cookies baked fresh daily.

GREEN ENVY ECO-BOUTIQUE
8 Franklin St., Newport, 401-619-1993
www.greenenvyshop.com
Open since 2008, this unique boutique is committed to offering only the most eco-friendly items available. Here you'll only find items produced in the USA by local artists or made by artisans in disadvantaged countries. Not only are the items in the boutique "green" but also the store is totally eco-friendly. Here you'll find beautiful gifts, soy candles, skin care and hair care products, jewelry, and other unique Made in the USA products. Gift certificates available.

LE PETIT GOURMET
26 Bellevue Ave, Newport, 401-619-3882
www.newportwinecellar.com
The sister shop to Newport Wine Cellar, this storefront offers a variety of gourmet treats including artisanal cheeses, gourmet prepared foods, fresh breads and a wide variety of epicurean delights.

THE MAGIC STUDIO
433 Thames St # 4, Newport, 401-841-0735
www.magicandpranks.com
This is Rhode Island's largest and only magic shop. Here you'll find top-notch magic sets, prank and gag gifts, juggling equipment and kites. A visit to this store is entertainment in itself.

MUSIC BOX
160 Thames St, Newport, 877-66-MUSIC
www.musicboxnewport.com
Founded in 1958, this locally owned company offers a unique variety of items including music, toys, games, sports memorabilia, candy, CDs, and vinyl records. If you can't find the music you want, they will order it for you.

NEWPORT FRUIT AND SMOOTHIE CO.
30 Bowen's Wharf, Newport
No phone or website
This family-owned shop has been making smoothies since 1999. Here you'll find a variety of dairy-free and vegan smoothies made with real fruit and no sugars. They also sell freshly squeezed lemonades, limeades, and orange juices.

NEWPORT SUNGLASS SHOP
BRICK MARKET PLACE
109 Swinburne Row, Newport, 401-841-9503
www.x-wear.com
This eyewear boutique is known as Newport's experts in sunglasses and eyewear. Hottest designer frames available like Smith Optics, Ray-Ban's, Oakley, and Maui Jim.

NEWPORT WINE CELLAR
24 Bellevue Ave, Newport, 401-619-3966
www.newportwinecellar.com
Since 2008, this unique shop offers a great selection of high quality, small production wines from all wine producing regions. Weekly wine tastings and

seminars are offered. Occasional offerings of craft beers.

PINK PINEAPPLE
380 Thames Rd, Newport, 401-619-0855
www.pinkpineappleshop.com
This boutique offers the Pink Pineapple cashmere collection designed by Stacie Hall. Here you'll find a beautiful selection of luxurious cashmere fashions as well as accessories, bracelets, and earrings.

PLEASANT SURPRISE
Brick Market Place
121 Swinburne Row, Newport, 401-846-1202
www.pleasant-surprise.com
Aptly named, this shop offers an eclectic mix of gifts, books, cards, toys, and home accessories. Most gift items have a nostalgic theme. Perfect place to buy a fun gift.
Shipping available.

ROCKPORT COMPANY STORE
240 Thames St, Newport, 401-849-9666
www.rockport.com
The Rockport Company has been providing shoes men's, women's and kid's dress and casual footwear since 1971. Besides shoes, you can also find a vast selection of accessories, socks, wallets, handbags, and belts.

TEN SPEED SPOKES
18 Elm St, Newport, 401-847-5609
www.tenspeedspokes.com
For more than 40 years this shop has been selling and servicing bicycles. This is a full-service bicycle shop that offers women's and men's clothing, shoes, sunglasses and accessories. Bicycle rentals available.

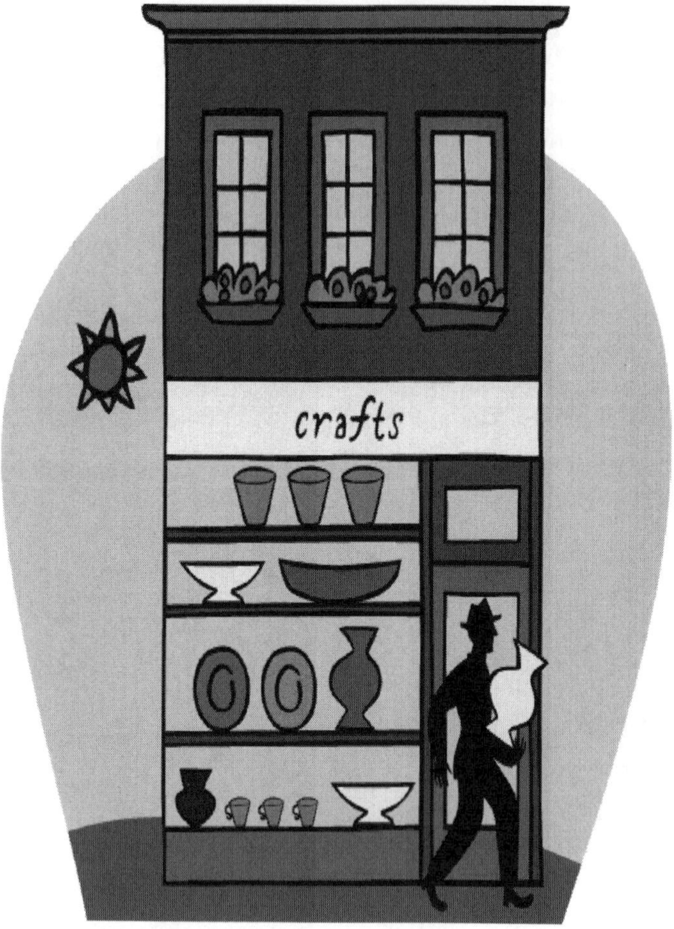
crafts

INDEX

2

22 BOWEN'S WINE BAR AND GRILL, 19

A

ADIRONDACK II, 37
ADMIRAL FITZROY INN, 10
ADVENTURE WATER SPORTS, 38
AIRBNB, 9
ALMONDY INN, 10
AQUIDNECK GROWERS WEDNESDAY FARMERS MARKET, 38
ARCHITECT'S INN, 11

B

BELLE'S CAFE, 19
BOOM BOOM ROOM, 33
BRAHMIN LEATHER WORKS, 49
BRETON POINT STATE PARK, 38
BRICK ALLEY PUB, 20
BRICK MARKET HISTORIC DISTRICT, 39
BRICK MARKET PLACE, 51, 52
BUSKERS IRISH PUB, 20

C

CABBAGE ROSE, 49
CASTLE HILL INN, 11
CHANLER, 27
Clark Cook House, 33
CLARKE COOKE HOUSE, 21
CLASSIC CRUISES, 39
CLIFF WALK, 39
CLIFFSIDE INN, 11
COOKIE JAR, 49

D

DECK, 22
DIEGO'S MEXICAN RESTAURANT, 22

F

FASTNET PUB, 33
FIFTH ELEMENT, 23
FLUKE WINE BAR & KITCHEN, 22
FORT ADAMS, 40
FORTY 1° NORTH, 12
FRANKLIN SPA, 23

G

GREEN ENVY ECO-BOUTIQUE, 50

H

HOTEL VIKING, 16
HOTWIRE, 9

I

INTERNATIONAL TENNIS HALL OF FAME, 40

J

JANE PICKENS THEATER, 41
JIMMY'S SALOON, 34

L

LE PETIT GOURMET, 50

M

M/V GANSETT, 42
MAGIC STUDIO, 50
MARSHALL SLOCUM GUEST HOUSE, 13
MIDTOWN OYSTER BAR, 24
MOORING SEAFOOD KITCHEN & BAR, 24
MUSEUM OF YACHTING, 41
MUSIC BOX, 51

N

NATIONAL MUSEUM OF AMERICAN ILLUSTRATION, 42
NAVAL WAR COLLEGE MUSEUM, 42
NEWPORT ART MUSEUM, 43
NEWPORT BEACH HOTEL, 13
NEWPORT BLUES CAFÉ, 34
NEWPORT CASINO, 40
NEWPORT DISTILLING COMPANY, 43
NEWPORT FRUIT AND SMOOTHIE, 51
NEWPORT GULLS, 44
NEWPORT MANSIONS, 46
NEWPORT MARRIOTT, 14
Newport Restoration Foundation, 48
NEWPORT SUNGLASS SHOP, 51
NEWPORT WINE CELLAR, 51
NORMAN BIRD SANCTUARY, 44

O

O'BRIEN'S PUB, 34
OCEAN DRIVE, 44
ONE PELHAM EAST, 34

P

PERRO SALADO, 25
PINK PINEAPPLE, 52
PLEASANT SURPRISE, 52
POUR JUDGEMENT, 25
Preservation Society of Newport County, 46
PRICELINE, 9

R

RED PARROT, 26
RHINO BAR & GRILLE, 27
ROCKPORT COMPANY STORE, 53
ROUGH POINT, 44, 48

S

SAMUEL WHITEHORNE HOUSE, 45
Service Life Tour, 47
SPICED PEAR, 27

T

TALLULAH ON THAMES, 28
TEN SPEED SPOKES, 53
THAMES STREET GUEST HOUSE, 15
TOURO SYNAGOGUE, 45

W

WHARF PUB, 29
WHITE HORSE TAVERN, 29

Other Books by the Same Author

Andrew Delaplaine has written in widely varied fields: screenplays, novels (adult and juvenile), travel writing, journalism. His books are available in quality bookstores as well as all online retailers.

Jack Houston St. Clair Political Thrillers

The Keystone File – Part 1
The Keystone File – Part 2
The Keystone File – Part 3
The Keystone File – Part 4
The Keystone File – Part 5
The Keystone File – Part 6
The Keystone File – Part 7 (final)

On Election night, as China and Russia mass soldiers on their common border in preparation for war, there's a tie in the Electoral College that forces the decision for President into the House of Representatives as mandated by the Constitution. The incumbent Republican President, working through his Aide for Congressional

Liaison, uses the Keystone File, which contains dirt on every member of Congress, to blackmail members into supporting the Republican candidate. The action runs from Election Night in November to Inauguration Day on January 20. Jack Houston St. Clair runs a small detective agency in Miami. His father is Florida Governor Sam Houston St. Clair, the Republican candidate. While he tries to help his dad win the election, Jack also gets hired to follow up on some suspicious wire transfers involving drug smugglers, leading him to a sunken narco-sub off Key West that has $65 million in cash in its hull.

THE RUNNING MATE
A Jack Houston St. Clair Political Thriller

Sam Houston St. Clair has been President for four long years and right now he's bogged down in a nasty fight to be re-elected. A Secret Service agent protecting the opposing candidate discovers that the candidate is sleeping with someone he shouldn't be, and tells his lifelong friend, the President's son Jack, this vital information so Jack can pass it on to help his father win the election. The candidate's wife has also found out about the clandestine affair and plots to kill the lover if her husband wins the election. Jack goes to Washington, and becomes involved in an international whirlpool of intrigue.

MARY FREEMAN SERIES
MIDNIGHT MASS - A Mary Freeman Thriller

Det. Lt. Mary Freeman stumbles upon a spectacular robbery of historic Trinity Church in downtown Manhattan on Christmas Eve, and after impressing the Mayor, gets assigned to the Task Force investigating the crime, throwing her headlong into a world of political intrigue and murder that rips apart every aspect of her life.

Jake Bricker Series

THE METER MAID MURDERS
A Jake Bricker Comic Thriller

A serial killer is loose on South Beach. But he's only killing meter maids, threatening the economic foundation of Miami Beach. Mayor Johnny Germane wants the killer caught NOW! But tall, dark and handsome Det. Sgt. Jake Bricker can't seem to nab the devious killer, even though he knows who the next victim will be. [Foul language; not for kids.]

The Adventures of Sherlock Holmes IV

In this series, the original Sherlock Holmes's great-great-great grandson solves crimes and mysteries in the present day, working out of the boutique hotel he owns on South Beach.

THE BORNHOLM DIAMOND

A mysterious Swedish nobleman requests a meeting to discuss a matter of such serious importance that it may threaten the line of succession in one of the oldest royal houses in Europe.

THE RED-HAIRED MAN

A man with a shock of red hair calls on Sherlock Holmes to solve the mystery of the Red-haired League.

THE CLEVER ONE

A former nun who, while still very devout, has renounced her vows so that she could "find a life, and possibly love, in the real world." She comes to Holmes in hopes that he can find out what happened to the man who promised to marry her, but mysteriously disappeared moments before their wedding.

THE COPPER BEECHES

A nanny reaches out to Sherlock Holmes seeking his advice on whether she should take a new position when her prospective employer has demanded that she cut her hair as part of the job.

THE MAN WITH THE TWISTED LIP

In what seems to be the case of a missing person, Sherlock Holmes navigates his way through a maze of perplexing clues that leads him through a sinister world to a surprising conclusion

THE DEVIL'S FOOT

Holmes's doctor orders him to take a short holiday in Key West, and while there, Holmes is called on to look into a case in which three people involved in a Santería ritual died with no explanation.

THE BOSCOMBE VALLEY MYSTERY

Sherlock Holmes and Watson are called to a remote area of Florida overlooking Lake Okeechobee to investigate a murder where all the evidence points to the victim's son as the killer. Holmes, however, is not so sure.

THE SIX NAPOLEONS

Inspector Lestrade calls on Holmes to help him figure out why a madman would go around Miami breaking into homes and businesses to destroy cheap busts of the French Emperor. It all seems very insignificant to Holmes—until, of course, a murder occurs.

The Trap Door Series

THE TRAP DOOR: THE "LOST" SCRIPT OF CARDENIO

A boy goes back to 1594 and Shakespeare's original Globe Theatre in search of a "lost" play by the world's greatest writer, and ends up embroiled in the plot to kill Queen Elizabeth the First and replace her with Mary, Queen of Scots. [Highly suitable for kids.]

The Annals Of Santopia

SANTOPIA: PART I, BOOK 1
SANTA & THE LOST PRINCESS

Three days before Christmas in the year 1900, Connie Claus has a son, and Santa names the boy Nicholas. Ameritus, Great Sage of Santopia, issues a Prophecy – the next girl born in the Kingdom will grow up to become Prince Nicky's Queen, and Nicky will become betrothed to her on his eighteenth birthday when he is invested as the future Santa at the Ritual of the Green Gloves. Far across Frozen Lake, the Baroness von Drear gives birth to a baby girl – she's overjoyed that her new baby will be the future Queen of Santopia. But when she discovers another girl was born just hours before her own to Taraxa and Inula, peasant family living in her Realm, she sets out to destroy them.

SANTOPIA: PART I, BOOK 2
SANTA & THE TRUTH REVEALED

It's Christmas Eve, and Elf Duncan journeys to the Other World as a stowaway on the Grand Sleigh. When discovered, he is forced to stay with the Red Elves in their Warren deep below the Tower of London until Santa can send a sleigh to bring him home. Back in Santopia during the same time period, Spicata rescues Taraxa and Inula from the carnivorous Pirandelves and gets them safely to Santopolis where he hopes to discover the real story behind the missing baby girl, thinking his reward would be great if he could get new information to the Baroness.

Screenplays

MIDNIGHT MASS – THE SCREENPLAY

Det. Lt. Mary Freeman stumbles upon a spectacular robbery of historic Trinity Church in downtown Manhattan on Christmas Eve, and after impressing the Mayor, gets assigned to the Task Force investigating the crime, throwing her headlong into a world of political intrigue and murder that rips apart every aspect of her life. (Based on the novel.)

MEETING SPENCER – THE SCREENPLAY

After a series of Hollywood flops, famed director Harris Chappell (Jeffrey Tambor in the movie released in 2012) returns to New York to relaunch his Broadway career. But Chappell's triumphant comeback begins to spiral out of control into a wild night of comic misadventure after meeting struggling actor Spencer (Jesse Plemons) and his old flame Didi (Melinda McGraw). This is an original script (not based on a novel or other source material). This is the original script, NOT the shooting script. You can stream the movie on Netflix. Or buy it on Amazon.

THE TRAP DOOR – THE SCREENPLAY

Looking for a famous "lost" play, a London boy performing in "A Midsummer Night's Dream" travels back in time to 1594 and the original production of the play in the original Globe Theatre. While there, he becomes embroiled in a plot to assassinate the Protestant Queen Elizabeth the First and replace her with the Catholic Mary, Queen of Scots. (Based on the novel.)

Delaplaine Travel Guides

Delaplaine Travel Guides represent the author's take on some of the many cities he's visited and many of which he has called home (for months or even years) during a lifetime of travel. The books are available as either ebooks or as printed books. Owing to the ease with which material can be uploaded, **both the printed and ebook editions** are updated 3 times a year.

The Long Weekend Series
Annapolis
Appalachicola
Atlanta
Austin
Berlin
Beverly Hills
Birmingham
Boston
Brooklyn
Cancún (Mexico)
Cannes
Cape Cod
Charleston
Charlotte
Chicago
Clearwater – St. Petersburg
Coral Gables
El Paso
Fort Lauderdale
Fort Myers & Sanibel
Gettysburg
Hilton Head
Hollywood – West Hollywood
Hood River (Ore.)
Jacksonville
Key West & the Florida Keys
London
Los Angeles / Downtown
Las Vegas
Louisville
Marseille
Martha's Vineyard
Memphis
Mérida (Mexico)
Mexico City
Miami & South Beach
Milwaukee
Myrtle Beach
Nantucket
Napa Valley
Naples & Marco Island
Nashville
New Orleans
New York / Brooklyn
Nee York / The Bronx
New York / Downtown

New York / Midtown
New York / Queens
New York / Upper East Side
New York / Upper West Side
Orlando & the Theme Parks
Palm Beach
Panama City (Fla.)
Paris
Pensacola
Philadelphia
Portland (Ore.)
Provincetown
Rio de Janeiro
San Francisco
San Juan
Santa Monica & Venice
Sarasota
Savannah
Seattle
Sonoma County
Tampa Bay
Venice (Calif.)
Washington, D.C.
West Hollywood & Hollywood

My niece, Senior Editor Sophie Delaplaine, has written several books on her own (besides her work in our Travel Department), and I thought you might like to know about them.

Made in the USA
Middletown, DE
13 June 2015